CW01046252

Theos – clear thinking on religion and society

Theos is the UK's leading religion and society think tank. With our ideas and content reaching media outlets with a combined circulation of 160 million in the past 5 years, we are shaping the hearts and minds of opinion formers about the role of faith in contemporary society by means of high quality research, events and media commentary. We provide a credible, informed and gracious Christian voice in our mainstream public conversations.

The *Economist* calls us "an organisation that demands attention", and Julian Baggini, the influential atheist philosopher, has said "Theos provides rare proof that theology can be interesting and relevant even – perhaps especially – for those who do not believe."

To learn more, check us out on social media:

twitter.com/theosthinktank | facebook.com/theosthinktank | www.theosthinktank.co.uk

Why we exist

Religion has emerged as one of the key public issues of the 21st century, both nationally and globally. Our increasingly religiously-diverse society demands that we grapple with religion as a significant force in public life. Unfortunately, much of the debate about the role and place of religion has been unnecessarily emotive and ill-informed. We exist to change that.

We reject the notion of any possible 'neutral' perspective on these issues. We also reject the idea that religion is a purely private matter or that it is possible to divide public and private values for anyone.

We seek, rather, to recognise and analyse the ethical ideas and commitments that underlie public life and to engage in open and honest public debate, bringing the tradition of Christian social and political thought to bear on current issues. We believe that the mainstream Christian tradition has much to offer for a flourishing society.

What we do

Theos conducts research, publishes reports, and holds debates, seminars and lectures on the intersection of religion, politics and society in the contemporary world. We also provide regular comment for print and broadcast media and briefing and analysis to parliamentarians and policy makers. To date, Theos has produced over 50 research reports focusing on the big issues impacting British society, including welfare (*The Future of Welfare: A Theos Collection*), law (*"Speaking Up" – Defending and Delivering Access to Justice Today*), economics (*Just Money: How Catholic Social Teaching can Redeem Capitalism*), multiculturalism (*Making Multiculturalism Work*) and voting reform (*Counting on Reform*), as well as on a range of other religious, legal, political and social issues.

In addition to our independently-driven work, Theos provides research, analysis and advice to individuals and organisations across the private, public and not-for-profit sectors. Our staff and consultants have strong public affairs experience, an excellent research track record and a high level of theological literacy. We are practised in research, analysis, debate, and media relations.

Where we sit

We are committed to the traditional creeds of the Christian faith and draw on social and political thought from a wide range of theological traditions. We also work with many non-Christian and non-religious individuals and organisations.

Theos was launched with the support of the Archbishop of Canterbury and the Cardinal Archbishop of Westminster, but it is independent of any particular denomination. We are an ecumenical Christian organisation, committed to the belief that religion in general and Christianity in particular has much to offer for the common good of society as a whole. We are not aligned with any point on the party political spectrum, believing that Christian social and political thought cuts across these distinctions.

Join the discussion by becoming a Friend of Theos

Impact how society views Christianity and shape the cultural debate

The Friends' Programme is designed specifically for people who wish to enter the heart of the current debate. When you join, our commitment is to keep you informed, equipped, encouraged and inspired so that you can be a voice in the public square with us.

As a member of the Friends' Programme, we provide you:

- *Hard copies of all our latest reports* on the most pressing issues – social justice, welfare, politics, spirituality, education, money, atheism, humanism…
- *Free access to our events.* Theos hosts a number of high calibre speakers (e.g. Rowan Williams, Larry Siedentop, Grace Davie) and debates ('Magna Carta and the future of liberty', 'Does humanism need Christianity?'). As a friend, you will receive invitations to all these without charge.
- *A network of like-minded people* who wish to share ideas and collaborate with one another. We host networking events which help you meet fellow Friends and build your own network, allowing ideas to flow and connections to form.
- *Our monthly e-newsletter* which is your one-stop digest for the latest news regarding religion and society.
- **If you join as an Associate**, you are *invited to private functions with the team*, allowing you to discuss upcoming projects, review the latest issues and trends in society, and have your say in where you see the public debate is going.

You can become a Friend or Associate today by visiting our website
www.theosthinktank.co.uk

If you'd prefer additional information, you can write to us directly:
Friends Programme, Theos, 77 Great Peter Street, London, SW1P 2EZ

If you have any inquiries regarding the Programme, you can email us at:
friends@theosthinktank.co.uk

The problem of proselytism

Published by Theos in 2015
© Theos

ISBN 978-0-9931969-1-1

For further information and subscription details please contact:

Theos
Licence Department
77 Great Peter Street
London
SW1P 2EZ

T 020 7828 7777
E hello@theosthinktank.co.uk
www.theosthinktank.co.uk

contents

acknowledgements

I would like to thank the many people who have already assisted with this research project, along with those who will continue to do so in the future as we work through its full practical application.

In particular, I am grateful to those people who consented to be interviewed on what can be a controversial and difficult subject, and for those who were gracious enough to take time to comment on drafts, including Andy Walton, Jonathan Chaplin, Jon Kuhrt and Helen Cameron. My colleagues Elizabeth Oldfield and Nick Spencer have helped developed and refine the argument over the course of the project, and Hannah Malcolm contributed background research during her time as a Theos intern. This reports limitations, however, are my own.

Paul Bickley

executive summary

The term proselytism has become a problem. The word, which traditionally simply meant the attempt to persuade someone to change their religion, has come to imply improperly forcing, bribing or taking advantage of vulnerabilities in the effort to recruit new religious adherents.

Those opposed to public faith argue that the threat of proselytising activity is one of the key reasons why faith-based organisations should not have a greater public role, engage in closer partnerships with statutory agencies or receive public funding. Even at a time of retrenchment in welfare spending, which has seen more and different groups involved in the delivery of public services, many public representatives and service commissioners still cite religious proselytism as a barrier to closer relationships with faith-based agencies.

There is, however, little evidence of widespread abuses. The vast majority of churches and religious charities decry activities which might be described as 'proselytising'. If anything, they experience pressures which can prevent them from maintaining a strong religious ethos and offering services which give due regard to spiritual care. Why, then, are concerns about proselytism so persistent? How should faith-based agencies respond?

In this report we address three key arguments that suggest that it is problematic for faith-based organisations to retain a strong and public religious character, and argue that they are not sufficient to restrict religious public, social and welfare action:

- Proselytism is a form of incivility

  The argument: in an increasingly secular society, proselytism in public environments is deeply inappropriate – a form or incivility. The problem of proselytism is that religious groups prioritise their needs and aspirations over the wider public good. At best, questioning the religious beliefs of others is irritating; at worst, it is uniquely divisive. In order to avoid unwelcome proselytising, faith-based organisations should not play a significant role in public services. When and if they do, they should restrain themselves from any tangible expression of faith.

We say: religious denominations and faith-based organisations do and should recognise that the condition of public engagement is prioritising the public good. However, civility is best recognised not when individuals and organisations are silent about their beliefs, but when they express them openly and respectfully, and when others are encouraged to do the same.

- Proselytism threatens minority groups

The argument: historically, Muslim and Christian proselytism have been responsible for damaging and fatally undermining indigenous traditions. In a contemporary context, they threaten minority religious and other identities. The problem of proselytism is not so much that of the advocacy of religious beliefs, but the advocacy of controversial – or even un-British – social, political or ethical norms. Proselytism of this kind should be resisted and controlled through force of law.

We say: minority groups often need protection, but this argument can be and is being used by privileged public and religious authorities that want to further entrench their position, thus undermining religious freedom. Religious mission can be and has been a component of cultural imperialism, but it can also resist and challenge it. Affirming and defending the dignity and integrity of ethnic and religious groups does not necessitate a full-blown religious pluralism or relativism. The right to choose one's own religion is a right recognised in many international agreements, including in Article 9 of the ECHR. Without open religious exchange that right becomes a 'dead letter'.

- Proselytism takes advantage of vulnerabilities

The argument: religious proselytisers are on the look-out for easy targets – those that are particularly gullible, or those that are in particular need. Religious charity is often delivered on the condition that beneficiaries at least give attention to the message of the provider, if not accept it. The problem of proselytism is the problem of the exercise of power. When they get to deliver public services, faith-based agencies use their position to purvey their religious beliefs amongst captive audiences.

We say: there are instances where religious agencies have taken advantage of people in a vulnerable position. The vast majority of religious voices are clear that there is no justification for making the provision of aid or assistance conditional on expressing religious beliefs. In the domestic context faith-based agencies are often commended by their users for an unconditional approach, whereas even state-based agencies commonly expect people to comply with certain conditions if they are to receive support. It's right to acknowledge vulnerability, which will be a more or less important consideration depending on the context, but an approach which 'vulnerable-ises' will result in a failure to take proper account of spiritual needs.

In interviews with statutory and faith-based organisation representatives we sought to explore the issues set out above in a practical context. These confirm that 'proselytism' continues to be a concern for statutory agencies, though we found little evidence of abuse.

None of the agencies we spoke to wanted to proselytise, where that meant using dishonest or coercive methods to win adherents. Indeed, many interviewees expressed their own concerns around 'proselytism' – they felt this implied taking rather than giving, and offended theological principles around the dignity of the individual and failed to prioritise the needs of the service user.

Faith-based organisations sought to realise their religious ethos in different ways. These ranged from agencies and services that focused on individual transformation and for whom participation in a faith community was an important part of their approach, to charities for whom ethos was explicitly articulated amongst senior leadership, but only experienced in a 'soft' way externally.

Agencies of different kinds can be thought of as taking what we call 'full fat', 'half fat' and 'low fat' approaches to including their faith in the service they provide.

- Full fat: it's not possible to abstract changes in belief and membership of a faith community from the 'service' in question. They seek to benefit the community through realising transformative individual change, usually at a small scale. These agencies tend not to seek or be in receipt of public funding. Success looks like the 'restoration' of the individual to the point where they can sustain their life, albeit with the support of a wider community. Faith participation is core to their identity and offer, but these agencies still seek to operate within the boundaries of 'informed consent'.

- Half fat: these services are embedded with or delivered in close partnership with a worshipping community. They aspire to be open to all, and seek to operate with a 'holistic' idea of mission – seeing social problems, and their solutions, as including biological, psychological, relational and spiritual factors. Success looks like resolving material, social and spiritual needs. They acknowledge the potential vulnerability of service users, but will seek to offer and share faith and participation in the life of a worshipping community, though they seek to offer a service which is unconditional and non-discriminatory.

- Low fat: for theological and ideological reasons, these organisations highly value inclusion. They disavow proselytism or overt evangelism as such, but will see their service users on a spiritual journey on which they can assist, though in reactive ways such as chaplaincy. These groups are more likely to be in receipt of statutory funding, and therefore are subject to and aware of greater regulatory and performance pressures. Success means delivering against targets set within contracts and agreements in ways richly informed by their faith-ethos, adding an extra dimension to the service.

conclusion and recommendations

Religious public action, like all public action, does need to be held accountable. Faith-based organisations (FBOs) in particular should acknowledge appropriate legal, regulatory or contractual limitations, as well as what counts for 'best practice'. In fact, the vast majority already do.

Accusations of proselytism tend to be attempts to restrict faith-based public action, rather than holding it accountable. This could be self-defeating, distracting stakeholders from a focused and practical conversation between commissioners and service providers about what is and isn't appropriate in given contexts.

We recommend:

- That government agencies and others avoid the language of proselytism; it is virtually impossible to define, let alone neutrally.

- That public agencies and FBOs should recognise that there are different approaches which will require different types of relationships with statutory agencies. This will help faith-based organisations move away from a binary approach, where more evangelical agencies tend to work 'off the radar', while those who want to work closely with other agencies are only seen as legitimate if their religious ethos is implicit and internal.

- In offering the full-, half-, and low-fat typology, we're do not seek to create hierarchy, or suggest that one approach will be right across all cases. Rather, the best practice emerges when FBOs are intentional, honest, explicit and consistent in their approach, rooted in a clear understanding of what they are trying to achieve. Clarity is the basis for relationships of trust between FBOs and funders, commissioners, peer organisations and service users. FBOs should speak more about the kind of organisation that they are, rather than the kind of organisation that they aren't.

- People are 'spiritual animals', and many services should recognise this to a greater degree. It's right that FBOs acknowledge vulnerability, but they shouldn't talk themselves into a position where it's impossible to recognise the spiritual aspect of people's life and experience. Agencies – faith-based and otherwise, and at whatever point on the full-, half-, or low-fat scale – can and should incorporate spiritual care into the services they hope to offer.

If we understand it properly and respond to it maturely, the problem of proselytism should be recognised for what it is – no problem at all.

introduction

In January 2015, the Department of Communities and Local Government launched a bidding process for a £400,000 grant to help strengthen faith institutions.[1] The successful organisation would help faith groups in "finding suitable training, advice or support when needed, sharing best practice, engaging with women and young people and having strong links with the wider community".

The specification document was admirably clear on the matter of restrictions. The money could not be spent on "activities promoting a religious faith or belief; acquisition of religious objects" or "the cost of supporting religiously-employed personnel". Nor would public money "be provided to organisations that do not support British values including democracy, human rights, equality before the law, and participation in society". And in case anyone missed it: "Money cannot be used for capital expenditure or proselytising".

The DCLG bid documents were unsuccessful in assuaging the fears around the use of public money. The National Secular Society found it "laughable to think that money won't be spent on proselytising".[2] Both the original document and the National Secular Society response betray a suspicion that religious agencies that want to spread their message are inclined to do so through dishonourable means, not least by accessing public funds to maximise their reach. When it comes to faith, extra assurances seem to be required.

> When it comes to faith, extra assurances seem to be required.

the case for this project

The words 'proselytism' and 'proselytising' are "words that think for us".[3] We don't always know exactly what it – proselytism – entails, but we think we know that the religious are quite prone to it. We also think we know that it's 'organised', 'aggressive', involves 'targeting', 'forcing' and 'propaganda' and is usually aimed at 'vulnerable' individuals or groups. These words conjure images of missionaries exporting 'rice-Christianity' throughout the British Empire, of exchanging 'charity' for prayer and penitence, or of creepy televangelists not looking so much to grow their flock as their market share.

These rhetorical flourishes don't add much in terms of clarity, but the images resonate for a reason. There have been, and are to this day, abuses where individuals – religious and otherwise – look to get something out of those they purport to help under the cover of gift and charity. But the spectre of proselytism, often summoned by secular campaigners, gives the impression that it is typical practice amongst faith-based organisations (FBOs) – that they're all characterised by a desire to propagate their message by illegitimate means.

To add complexity, there are clearly different institutional contexts, times and functions where more or less explicit religious expression is appropriate. What a person can or ought to say on Speaker's Corner is different to what she can or ought to say if she's a chaplain, or a doctor. This is not that she stops believing these things when at work, but that she recognises she's performing a different function in those different contexts. We hear a lot about cases where that distinction seems to have broken down to a greater or lesser degree, but little about how those distinctions are understood or maintained by the religious.

When it comes to those who provider public services (or, for that matter, services to the public[4]) evidence of abuses, as opposed to anecdote, accusation and conjecture, are thin on the ground. Yet misunderstanding and anxiety around the desire, extent and ways in which religious organisations and individuals will seek to share their faith will, and already do, adversely affect their ability to work with others to engage in the delivery of services to the public and work for the common good. On the other side, FBOs that want to participate more in delivering services to the public are often unsure about what is acceptable, appropriate or possible in terms of retaining and articulating their faith-based ethos, and therefore 'self-secularise', leaving their organisation with an 'identity crisis'.

This is having real and negative outcomes.

First, groups that could contribute effectively to the common good will not necessarily do so if they are distrusted, or required to offer assurances above and beyond those which other providers would have to give. The resources which faith groups offer – human, social and physical capital – could ultimately be lost to the wider community. In short, there's a 'chill' effect around the prospect of working with FBOs.

Second, FBOs could fail to serve their communities in ways that take their service users' faiths, beliefs and spiritualities seriously. Fear-mongering around proselytism could replace diversity with uniformity, limiting organisations to nothing more than a vague sense of organisational 'ethos'. The field of 'spiritual

> *'Spiritual care' is clearly one of the areas where FBOs could genuinely add value.*

care' is clearly one of the areas where FBOs could genuinely add value above and beyond secular providers – they should be doing more of this, not less.

Third, government could end up 'asset stripping' FBOs, using their human, social and physical capital while de-legitimising their motivation to serve people in a holistic way, and therefore ultimately undermining them.

Alternatively, if fears around proselytism are well founded – if there were evidence of abuse of public funds and/or positions of public trust by religious institutions, or if faith groups were clearly motivated to serve their communities only in order to create a platform for evangelistic activities – then statutory authorities would rightly exercise caution when working with FBOs and look to ensure that proper safeguards were put in place.

This report attempts to address precisely those issues, but to do so we also have to identify and investigate both the approach of FBOs and the ways in which the word proselytism is used. It is what is supposed to make working with FBOs particularly risky, but it is rarely set out clearly exactly what proselytism is supposed to be – the word is doubly problematic because it is both used tendentiously and defined subjectively.

the structure and methods of this report

This report seeks to explore the social and political context which makes overt expression of faith, and attempts to convert others, particularly problematic. It offers insight into how FBOs can negotiate the challenges of concretely embodying and expressing a faith-based ethos, asks whether the concerns of partners and commissioners are well founded, and suggests measures that could contribute to the development of a practical framework where FBOs are enabled to participate on the right terms.

After looking at the vexed issue of definition in Chapter 1, the report explores three key arguments against proselytism. In Chapter 2, we observe that in an increasingly irreligious society, where there is considerable cultural discomfort with orthodox religious belief, proselytism is seen as a form of incivility. In Chapter 3, we explore how in the context of religious diversity – globally and locally – proselytism is perceived as being particularly threatening to minority religious groups. In Chapter 4, we address how, at a time of increased supply of and increased demand for faith-based services, the issue of vulnerability makes any form of overt religious profession deeply problematic.

We do not seek to ignore or minimise the concerns. Instead, we will engage with them critically, and ask whether they are balanced critiques of public faith, and how such problems might be practically mitigated in the British context.

We explore these questions mainly in the context of the growing role of FBOs in welfare provision (rather than, for example, religious expression in the workplace). Therefore, we have not just explored them in theory, but also in the light of the practice of FBOs and the experience and approach of service commissioners. In preparing this report, we have conducted twenty three confidential one-to-one interviews with service commissioners, representatives of FBOs and others who have looked at the way FBOs make their faith-based identity concrete. We don't claim that these interviews are fully representative of all aspects of the 'faith-sector'. Rather, our objective here was to explore practice 'on the ground', and to ask how commissioners think about the subject – what has their experience of working with FBOs been? What are their concerns?

We selected a range of agencies, including some who have signed self-denying ordinances when it comes to proselytism, ranging through to agencies for whom changes in lifestyle, beliefs, behaviour and belonging were central to their service model. In what follows, we will observe and affirm a variegated approach amongst FBOs. Some are 'full fat' in nature, and rely on religious conversion and participation in a religious community as a core part of the service, while others are 'half fat' or even 'low fat', where faith might closely inform an organisation's ethos but would only implicitly influence the service being delivered. These different types of service all have a place, though they will have different kinds of relationships with service users, peer organisations and statutory commissioners/funders. These results of these interviews are detailed throughout the report.

Different types of services all have a place, though they will have different kinds of relationships with service users, peer organisations and statutory commissioners/funders.

In the conclusion, we will make recommendations for action. In their desire to build confidence amongst commissioners, some faith-based organisations rule out proselytism in charters, covenants and other public statements. Instead, we will consider questions about the appropriate ways in which faith should be incorporated into their public interactions. Our overall argument is for self-disciplined religious public action, where overt religious expression isn't prevented but pursued responsibly.

other recent work on this subject

There is a large body of literature addressing the theme of proselytism. This includes historical and contemporary analyses of the combination of religious missionary activity with military and political power, whether in the colonial period or in the activities of missionaries in newly opening post-communist states.[5] Other work deals with the alleged combination of proselytism with international aid and development, or the place of evangelism as an aspect of religious freedom. This report touches on some of this work below.

Of more direct and practical concern are debates around the role of FBOs in the delivery of public services. If religious organisations seek to proselytise in their own time, using their own resources, then that is one thing. If they do so while performing public functions in a religiously diverse society, taking the public pound, is another.

Recent relevant studies include:

- Professor Sarah Johnsen's 2011 study into faith-based homeless services, funded by the ESRC/AHRC Religion and Society Programme, found that only a small number of service users had experienced being proselytised, none of them in the context of publically funded services, and that service users were indifferent as to the faith affiliation of an agency, provided that services were not contingent on participation in religious activities and that workers respected their right not to be subjected to faith-based conversations.[6]

- A 2013 report on faith and spirituality in homelessness services, written by (atheist) Carwyn Gravell for the consultancy Lemos and Crane, argued that a secular orthodoxy had emerged in the homelessness sector, making it difficult for service users to find forums in which they could discuss, engage with and explore their faith. The report recommended that person-centred providers should give greater attention to the spirituality of service users, including linking them up with local places of worship and setting up spirituality discussion groups.[7]

- The 2013 ResPublica report, *Holistic Mission: Social Action and the Church of England* found that 81 per cent of respondents to a survey of Church of England congregations said that they help others because of their faith, but argued that faith was not a motivation for partisanship or sectarianism; and 88 per cent of respondents said that they felt comfortable helping people who have different values or religious beliefs. The report called for the Church of England to "accept and dispel" concerns around proselytization when competing for government contracts.[8]

- The Evangelical Alliance *Faith in the Community Report*, published in 2013, which included data collected through an extensive survey of local authorities, found that respondents suggested fears around exclusivity, equality and diversity and proselytization continued to be a barrier to working more closely with faith groups. The report noted that although respondents articulated concerns that, for instance, faith-based service providers might only work within their own faith community, they tended not to support the claims with examples.[9]

- The Demos report, *Faithful Providers*, again published in 2013, observed that the "censorious language around 'proselytism'… gives faith-based organisations the impression that there is something offensive about their deep moral commitments". The study, which included interviews with a selection of around twenty FBOs, found no evidence of "aggressive proselytising or of discrimination on grounds of faith" and argued that "there should be no objection to providers of public services discussing their faith with service users who express an interest", but suggested that "aggressive proselytization" should be avoided.[10]

- The recent Equality and Human Rights Commission call for evidence report, *Religion or belief in the workplace and service delivery*, found that some respondents reported that they had be subjected to "unwelcome preaching or proselytising" or senior staff seeking to proselytise junior staff: "Atheists and Humanists in particular described 'relentless and unwelcomed preaching' from colleagues". A social care project, jointly operated by a Christian and a secular charity, reported some friction: "the secular charity made complaints to the Christian charity about the expression of religious views during service provision and stated that religion should not be talked about except in designated rooms". Christian charities reported suspected discrimination around funding and other issues. They felt that they were held to be unwilling or unable to serve the whole of the community, including people of other religions or no religion, and those from the LGBT community.[11]

These reports affirm the case for research. First, there continues to be a perception – particularly amongst statutory authorities – that proselytism might be a problem when it comes to faith-based providers. Second, they show that rumours of proselytization are greatly exaggerated. Third, they suggest in fact that service users do not benefit from the 'secular orthodoxy' that faith needs to be taken out of the services offered to vulnerable client groups – indeed, greater attention needs to be paid to allowing for the spirituality and spiritual needs of service users.

references – introduction

1   Department of Communities and Local Government, 'Strengthening faith institutions' programme bidding documents. Available at https://www.gov.uk/government/publications/ strengthening-faith-institutions-programme-bidding-documents (accessed 13.08.15).

2   National Secular Society, "£400,000 Government scheme to 'strengthen' faith organisations in Britain". Available at http://www.secularism.org.uk/news/2015/02/gbp400000-government-scheme-to-strengthen-faith-organisations-in-britain (accessed 13.08.15).

3   To borrow the title of Edward Skidelsky's column in Prospect Magazine. See, for instance, Edward Skidelski, 'Beyond Inappropriate', *Prospect Magazine*, December 2009. Available at http://www.prospectmagazine.co.uk/regulars/words-that-think-for-us (accessed 18.08.2015).

4   Here, I'm using 'public services' to denote publicly-funded welfare services, as opposed to welfare activities provided for the general public but funded privately – which I call here 'services to the public'.

5   Survival International still list Christian missionaries as one of the threats to uncontacted tribes. See http://www.survivalinternational.org/articles/3106-uncontacted-tribes-the-threats (accessed 19.08.2015).

6   Sarah Johnsen, 'Case study 6: The role of faith-based organisations in service provision for homeless people', in Linda Woodhead and Rebecca Cato eds., *Religion and Change in Modern Britain* (Routledge, 2012), pp. 295-298.

7   Carwyn Gravell, *Lost and Found: faith and spirituality in the lives of homeless people*, Lemos and Crane (2013). Available at https://www.lemosandcrane.co.uk/lemos&crane/index. php?id=217018 (accessed 19.08.2015).

8   James Noyes, *Holistic Mission: Social Action and the Church of England*, ResPublica (2013).

9   *Faith in the Community: Strengthening ties between faith groups and local authorities*, Evangelical Alliance (2013).

10 Jonathan Birdwell, *Faithful Providers*, Demos (2013).

11 Martin Mitchell, Kelsey Beninger, Alice Donald and Erica Howard, *Religion or belief in the workplace and service delivery: Findings from a call for evidence*, NatCen Social Research/Equality and Human Rights Commission (2015). Available from http://www. equalityhumanrights.com/sites/default/files/publication_pdf/RoB%20Call%20for%20 Evidence%20Report.pdf (accessed 19.08.2015).

the problem of definition

At the start of any such report, it is sensible to clarify the definition of important terms. It just so happens, on this occasion, that the lack of definition is a large part of the problem.

For the National Secular Society, the distinction between faith groups "increasing their reach in society and proselytism is a fine one". Here proselytism means intentional extension of profile or influence. In France, the 2004 statute preventing pupils in schools and colleges wearing religious dress was described by the then Assembly Speaker, Jean-Louis Debré, as a "clear affirmation that public school is a place for learning and not for militant activity or proselytism".[1] Here proselytism means any outward display of religious identity at all.

In contrast to these broad uses, where proselytism relates to any activity where religion is explicit (and therefore inappropriate!), the word proselytism is sometimes used by religious commentators to describe inappropriate tactics in religious advocacy. In recent high profile comments, Pope Francis declared during an annual week of prayer for Christian unity that "our shared commitment to proclaiming the Gospel enables us to overcome proselytism and competition in all their forms".[2] He has also called proselytism "solemn nonsense",[3] while also maintaining that "missionary outreach is paradigmatic for all the Church's activity". He clearly means something very different to those who use the word proselytism to denote any and every form of religious communication.

> The word proselytism is sometimes used by religious commentators to describe inappropriate tactics.

What, precisely, does the term 'proselytism' describe?

legal definitions

Perhaps we can look to the law for guidance? We might anticipate that those jurisdictions – of which there are a considerable number even in western contexts – which seek to control proselytism might have legislation that is capable of being clearly applied by courts.

The case of Kokkinakis v. Greece (Application no. 14307/88) in the European Court of Human Rights is the most notable legal judgement in this area.[4] Mr Minos Kokkinakis, a Jehovah's Witness living in Sitia, Greece, had already been arrested on no less than 60 occasions for offences relating to proselytism.[5] In 1986, he was arrested after a 15 minute conversation with a neighbour and convicted of attempting "to intrude on the religious beliefs of Orthodox Christians, with the intention of undermining those beliefs, by taking advantage of their inexperience, their low intellect and their naivety". He was sentenced to four months' imprisonment, convertible into a pecuniary penalty of 400 drachmas per day's imprisonment, and a fine of 10,000 drachmas. The conviction was upheld in two appeals, and Mr Kokkinakis appealed to the Commission in 1988 on the basis that his conviction was in breach of the rights secured in Articles 7, 9, 10 and 14 of the European Convention on Human Rights.

In his case, Mr Kokkonakis:

> pointed to the logical and legal difficulty of drawing an even remotely clear dividing-line between proselytism and freedom to change one's religion or belief and, either alone or in community with others, in public and in private, to manifest it, which encompassed all forms of teaching, publication and preaching between people.

He criticised the absence of any description of the "objective substance" of the offence of proselytism and pointed to the risk of its "extendibility" by police, given that the relevant Greek legislation included terms like "in particular" and "indirect" proselytism.

The court reached its judgement in 1993, with much of the judgement turning on the definitions of proselytism offered in Greek law – specifically Article 13 of the Greek Constitution and law 1363/1938. Substantially, the court argued that Article 9 includes in principle the right to try to convince one's neighbour, for example through teaching. If that's not permitted, then the freedom to change [one's] religion or belief, enshrined in Article 9, would be likely to "remain a dead letter".

However, the court itself wanted to make a distinction between "bearing Christian witness and improper proselytism", and acknowledged that the later could be limited with a view to protecting the religious freedom of others in a democratic society.[6] The Greek laws against proselytism were acceptable "in so far as they are designed only to punish improper proselytism".[7] The fault of the Greek courts, and the breach in Article 9, had been in failing to demonstrate that Mr Kokkonakis had actually gone about his proselytising in an improper way.

What was to be considered improper? For the distinction itself, the Court had drawn on a 1956 World Council of Churches document, but the Court did not consider it necessary "to define in the abstract" what improper might mean – though the Greek law did offer hints. In separate opinions, some judges argued that the Greek case was problematic, relying on too vague concepts such as

> proselytism that is not respectable… giving the State the possibility of arrogating to itself the right to assess a person's weakness in order to punish a proselytiser, an interference that could become dangerous if resorted to by an authoritarian State.[8]

Two things might be drawn from the above. First, the European Court of Human Rights is clear – Article 9 includes the right to share one's faith. Second, the Court found that this freedom might be controlled in law when it comes to 'improper' proselytism, but the Court did not find it necessary to define that in an abstract way. For this distinction, the Kokkanikas judgement relies upon distinctions drawn from *theological* rather than legal sources – specifically, those made by the World Council of Churches. In essence, the Court recognised that proselytising abuses are a possibility, but that setting strict legal boundaries was difficult, referring onto documents which reflect attempts at religious self-regulation. It is to these we now turn.

The European Court of Human Rights is clear – Article 9 includes the right to share one's faith.

religious definitions

It is hard to think of any religious individual or organisation that would willingly use the language of proselytism to describe their own activity – Muslims would refer to Da'wah, Christians to mission, evangelism and witness.[9] Even within these, one could explore various different modes and models, which are often in held in tension with one another having evolved depending on the theological starting place and the social and political context.[10] Not all forms of public witness or action are intended solely to bring about individual conversions.

Largely, however, proselytism is a term used by religious commentators to describe corrupted forms of religious witness. Consider the following quote from the 2005 Papal Encyclical, *Deus Caritas Est*.

> Charity, furthermore, cannot be used as a means of engaging in what is nowadays considered proselytism. Love is free; it is not practised as a way of achieving other ends. But this does not mean that charitable activity must somehow leave God

and Christ aside. For it is always concerned with the whole man. Often the deepest cause of suffering is the very absence of God. Those who practice charity in the Church's name will never seek to impose the Church's faith upon others…[11]

Similarly, Pope Francis' apostolic exhortation, *Evangelii Gaudium* argues that "it is not by proselytism that the church grows, but by attraction", distinguishing between "the imposition of obligations" and "to invite others to a delicious banquet".[12] The extended processes of ecumenical dialogue led by bodies like the World Council of Churches have reached similar conclusions to the Roman Catholic Church – proselytism is usually taken to describe distorted and unworthy approaches to religious witness.[13]

Critics, however, might argue that by disavowing proselytism whilst simultaneously insisting that charity can't "leave God and Christ aside", the religious are deliberately creating grey areas. Both the encyclical and the exhortation identify the need to be concerned with the "whole man", and are clear that "Christians have the duty to proclaim the Gospel without excluding anyone" – wouldn't that count as proselytism for most people? Even well-disposed commentators have argued that the definitions between, for example, 'evangelism' and 'mission' and 'proselytism' are either too subtle or too arbitrary for a broad audience – "better to use the same word to describe the same phenomenon, and then distinguish between moral and immoral expressions of this phenomenon".[14]

> Faith should indeed be offered to others, but in ways which are humble, generous, respectful, honest and free.

It's important to note that, in refusing the term, churches and FBOs are not attempting to obfuscate, using different words to talk about what everyone else calls proselytism, thereby dodging secular bullets. Rather, they are engaged in an ongoing conversation around the ethics of evangelism and witness in plural societies. In the same way that there are forms of secular persuasion – dishonest advertising, for example – that transgress ethical boundaries, religious traditions take the view that there are things that they should not do. They take this view not because they have adopted the secular perspective that public religion is a problem. Rather, it is because their theologically informed understanding is that their faith should indeed be offered to others, but in ways which are humble, generous, respectful, honest and free. This type of religious advocacy is orientated to the good of the other, not for the good of the missionary or his or her institution.

So it was with the agencies and individuals we spoke to about the question of proselytism. All bore a strong faith identity and were highly motivated by their religious convictions, though they incorporated this into their practice in very different ways. What was common to them all, however, is that none warmed to the language of proselytism. They were either not particularly familiar with it, or suspected that it was unhelpfully pejorative, implying some attempt at forcing, harassing, or stepping beyond the boundaries of consent, where their professed objective was the good of the other. One interviewee, while herself concerned by the possibility of proselytism by FBOs, felt that it was wrong to single out religious individuals – that there were lots of people 'with an agenda'.

statutory perspectives

In order to understand statutory perspectives on these issues, we conducted a number of confidential one-to-one interviews with people working in public agencies, specifically those who might work with or commission faith groups. Amongst other things, these interviews sought to explore understandings of what might constitute improper proselytism.

For the main part, statutory interviewees were eager to work more with faith-based organisations and saw many advantages in doing so. One suggested that FBOs, an ignored sub-group within the wider third sector, had not benefitted from the same degree of capacity building and proactive partnership development, and therefore deserved some over-due attention. Several spoke about how the Equality Act was a motivating factor in seeking to do more with FBOs, since 'religion and belief' is a protected characteristic.

However, there is often a perception that extensive engagement with FBOs is complex and risky. One council officer – albeit working for an authority which had already established an infrastructure around faith engagement – said "There was a feeling of, 'why are we having to get involved in this? It's going to cause us a lot of problems'". This interviewee spoke of a contested environment, where some colleagues felt strongly that state agencies should remain secular.

> *There is often a perception that extensive engagement with FBOs is complex and risky.*

A desire to avoid sponsoring proselytism was one of the issues in play for statutory interviewees, though one part of a wider gamut of difficulties. They generally accepted the term, though one indicated that he had to visit Wikipedia to see what it meant the first time he heard it! Activities which might raise concerns for them included explicit attempts to change the beliefs of individuals or seek to recruit them to a religious organisation, but also:

- activities that were focused on one religious group, and not open to other religious groups or the wider community;

- services of religious worship, or activities which took part on religious premises;

25

- the advocacy of controversial social or political views rooted in their religious faith;

- specific religious acts, such as praying for people or 'laying on of hands';

- services that should be open to all but were being delivered in a particularly religious way or using overly religious language;

- the use of public platforms, achieved under the pretence of offering a service, to advocate for their faith.

> *None of the interviewees were able to report actual historic examples of occasions when, for example, faith agencies had misspent public funding for the purposes of proselytization.*

Interviewees were not saying that all these things were wrong in themselves, just that they were not to occur in public spaces or as part of the discharge of some public function. Nor were they the business of statutory agencies. Tellingly, however, none of the interviewees were able to report actual historic examples of occasions when, for example, faith agencies had misspent public funding for the purposes of proselytization – "In all the time [I've been here] I've not come across any serious examples… It's more a perception of what could happen".

There are two possible interpretations of this fact – first, that it was an urban myth that had resulted in risk-aversion on the part of statutory agencies regarding working with FBOs or, second, that potential proselytisers were being weeded out before they were able to cross any 'red lines'.

Probably, there was a little of both going on – one interviewee specifically stated that they included principles of non-proselytising in their procurement and monitoring processes. Initiatives like the All Party Parliamentary Group on Faith and Society Covenant make similar commitments. However, one interviewee also reported that some council services refused to do things for 'bonkers reasons' (e.g., promote commemorations of the King James Bible), because they were concerned that this might be seen as proselytism.

What emerged from these interviews, therefore, was less a concern about evangelism or proselytism, than a range of concerns that were often grouped using the term proselytism. For instance, the vulnerability of potential service users was also cited as a significant factor. For others, to speak of proselytism brought up concerns around religious groups prioritising their own objectives over the needs of service-users.

> It's about putting aside your private gain – you know, "what's in it for me?" – and separating your own agenda from the needs of another person. The issue is, is this

in their public interests, and not in your private gain – there [should be] nothing in it that benefits you.

For others still, the concern was that their public role was to bring the community together, and offer protection for minority communities. Proselytism became problematic when it made those things more difficult to achieve.

There's a role for us in terms of bringing communities together, insomuch as it's not appropriate for proselytising to get in the way of our provision of goods and services… we do have a vested interest in communities living together in terms of [combatting] hate crime, homophobic bullying, [and] in promoting gender equality.

in summary

If proselytism is indeed a word that does our thinking for us, but it is also one with a meaning that is uncertain, then it comes as no surprise that thinking around the subject remains unclear. When used without definition, it can be pejorative and sometimes seems to mean little more than a collection of religious things we disapprove of. Indeed, part of our argument has been that this is deliberate – vague accusations that religious organisations will use public position or public money to proselytise are often simply a campaigning tactics used to block faith-based service providers from greater engagement.

That said, we should not deny that there might be genuine problems that have to be carefully negotiated. What is clear from the above is agreement in legal, religious and statutory contexts that there is scope for religious public expression, but that it has boundaries – it is these which we must now explore.

chapter 1 – references

1   "French MPs Vote to Ban Headscarves", *Sky News*, 10 February 2004. Available at http://news.
    sky.com/story/245721/french-mps-vote-to-ban-headscarves (accessed 19.08.2015)

2   Ann Schneible, "Christian unity demands encounter – not theory, says Pope", *Catholic News
    Agency*, 25 January 2015. Available at http://www.catholicnewsagency.com/news/christian-
    unity-demands-encounter-not-theory-says-pope-44011/ (accessed 18.08.2015).

3   Eugenio Scalfari, "The Pope: how the Church will change", *La Repubblica*, 1 October 2013.
    Available at http://www.repubblica.it/cultura/2013/10/01/news/pope_s_conversation_with_
    scalfari_english-67643118/ (accessed 18.08.2015).

4   European Court of Human Rights, Kokkinakis v. Greece (Application no. 14307/88), 1993.
    Available at http://hudoc.echr.coe.int/eng?i=001-57827#{"itemid":["001-57827"]} (accessed
    19.08.2015).

5   The judgement notes that, "under the reign of Otto I (1832-62), the Orthodox Church,
    which had long complained of a Bible society's propaganda directed at young Orthodox
    schoolchildren on behalf of the Evangelical Church, managed to get a clause added to the
    first Constitution (1844) forbidding 'proselytism and any other action against the dominant
    religion'. The Constitutions of 1864, 1911 and 1952 reproduced the same clause. The
    1975 Constitution prohibits proselytism in general". Ironically, the relevant article of the
    constitution bears the title 'freedom of religion'.

6   The limitations to Article 9 rights were subsequently explored, in connection with
    proselytism, in *Lautsi + others v Italy* (2009), which concerned the display of crucifixes on the
    walls of Italian classrooms. An initial judgment found "an obligation on the State to refrain
    from imposing beliefs, even indirectly, in places where persons were dependent on it". This
    judgement was in large part later contradicted by the Grand Chamber of the Court in 2011.

7   Section 2 of Law no. 1672/1939 describes proselytism as "any kind of inducement or promise
    of an inducement or moral support or material assistance, or by fraudulent means or by
    taking advantage of… inexperience, trust, need, low intellect or naïvety".

8   Partly concurring opinion of Judge Pettiti, *Kokkinakis v. Greece*, p. 21.

9   The word 'proselyte' is used with a specific meaning in the New Testament, that is to
    describe Gentile converts to Judaism, rather than those who follow 'the Way' – which is
    to say Christianity. The only reference to proselytism made by Jesus is far from flattering
    (Matthew 23.15), and the mandate that Jesus offers his disciples is not to proselytise but to be
    witnesses.

10 See, for instance, R. Scott Appleby and Angela J. Lederach, "Conversion, Witness, Solidarity
    and Dialogue: Modes of the Evangelizing Church in Tension", *The Review of Faith &
    International Affairs* 7:1, 2009 for an illustration of some of the distinctions that can be made.

11 Benedict XVI, *Deus Caritas Est* [*God is Love – On Christian Love*], 2005. Available at http://
    w2.vatican.va/content/benedict-xvi/en/encyclicals/documents/hf_ben-xvi_enc_20051225_

deus-caritas-est.html (accessed 19.08.2015). This is consistent with and a development of Second Vatican Council documents such as *Ad Gentes* and *Dignitatis Humanae*).

12 Francis, *Evangelii Gaudium* [*The Joy of the Gospel – On the Proclamation of the Gospel in Today's World*], 2013. Available at http://w2.vatican.va/content/francesco/en/apost_exhortations/documents/papa-francesco_esortazione-ap_20131124_evangelii-gaudium.html (accessed 18.08.2015).

13 See for instance the World Council of Churches joint working group document *Common Witness and Proselytism*, 1970, which offers the definition: "Here is meant improper attitudes and behavior in the practice of Christian witness. Proselytism embraces whatever violates the right of the human person, Christian or non-Christian, to be free from external coercion in religious matters, or whatever, in the proclamation of the Gospel, does not conform to the ways God draws free men to himself in response to his calls to serve in spirit and in truth". Available at http://www.pro.urbe.it/dia-int/jwg/doc/e_jwg-n3_06.html (accessed 19.08.2015). Other documents of an inter-confessional or inter-religious nature include *Christian Witness in a Multi-Religious World – Recommendations for Conduct* from the WCC, PCID, WEA and, closer to home, *Ethical Guidelines for Christian and Muslim Witness in Britain* from the UK Christian Muslim Forum.

14 Elmer John Thiessen, *The Ethics of Evangelism: A Philosophical Defence of Proselytising and Persuasion* (IVP Academic, 2011), p. 12. Thiessen advocates the adoption of a neutral definition: "The deliberate attempt of a person or an organisation through communication, to bring about the conversion of another person of groups of persons, where conversion is understood to involve a change to a person's belief, behaviour, identity and belonging".

the incivility of proselytism

Proselytism has not suddenly become controversial or unpopular, but there are contemporary factors which have made it particularly problematic.

Our society is one which is both more irreligious, with a growing discomfort with orthodox religious belief, and one which increasingly thinks in secular terms. Overt religious expression – particularly that which seeks to witness, preach or convert – is seen as particularly problematic, and the social and political authority of religious traditions is also disputed.

the religious 'market'

If we apply the (much disputed) analogy of the market to religious change, then we in the UK have moved from a situation of market dominance by the established Church of England, alongside a limited field of alternatives in dissenting, non-conformist Christian traditions, to a situation where there is no clear leading brand and a growing number of potential customers don't align at all. As recently as 1983, 40 per cent of respondents to the British Social Attitudes survey said that they were Anglican. The corresponding figure in 2014 was 17 per cent. Alongside that decline in Anglican identity, we have also become a more religiously diverse society, not least because of immigration from the Indian sub-continent and beyond.

A decline in religious identification results in religious groups seeking greater visibility.

We will explore some of the challenges of proselytism in a multicultural society in the next chapter – the point here is that religious change has arguably created the feeling of 'market conditions', where more evangelistic expressions of religious belief and practice have emerged. Ironically, a decline in religious identification results in religious groups seeking greater visibility. As the sociologist Peter Berger puts it:

> The religious tradition, which previously could be authoritatively imposed, now has to be marketed. It must be "sold" to a clientele that is no longer constrained

to "buy". The pluralist situation is, above all, a market situation. In it, the religious institutions become marketing agencies and the religious traditions become consumer commodities.[1]

In public perception, this places religious leaders and religious institutions on a par with salesman – always having to persuade potential customers of the benefits of their product, and even adjusting their 'services' to cater for perceived religious needs. And each salesman is competing with all the others, looking for competitive advantage or ways to get at potential customers.

It is questionable whether this accurately describes the mentality of many faith institutions, particularly those that seek, in a plural public square, to engage in charitable and caring initiatives (there are, after all, many forms of religious witness and interfaith engagement that do not have individual conversions as their goal). However, where such presumptions exist the state comes to be seen as the guarantor of a properly regulated religious market. The desire amongst religious institutions and FBOs to deliver public services or engage with their communities comes to be seen not as an attempt to serve the public good, but as a way of achieving their own objectives – in the case of proselytism, giving them a platform on which to present their message.

In this context, state agencies – even those who engage enthusiastically with FBOs – can be anxious to be seen as 'impartial' and 'neutral', if not explicitly 'secular', and the conditions for public engagement with religious

> *Proselytising incivility might not be necessarily religious in nature.*

organisations are tightly controlled. More than this, public secularism becomes the only feasible option – anything else is a failure to recognise contemporary diversity, and risks being deeply divisive. One statutory representative spoke of a struggle in convincing colleagues that a local authority should work more closely with FBOs.

> So there's always been a question about whether we're a secular organisation, when I've said that in rooms full of politicians I've very definitely been told that we are, but I've spoken to our corporate governance people who've told me there's absolutely nothing in our constitution at all. We're not a secular organisation… and we're not a religious organisation, but we're not a secular organisation…

public faith as incivility

This alleged failure of religious agencies to prioritise the public good means that public faith comes to be seen as a kind of 'incivility'.

Civility, according to Derek Edyvane, quoting Edward Shils, includes "patterns of conduct" and "particular attitudes towards others".[2] The term is much debated by political theorists: for some civility is a 'cold' virtue expressing deferred hostility, while for others it denotes 'warm' patterns of respect and even friendship. Here, we use the term incivility to describe two separate but interrelated complaints about proselytism.

In the first sense, religious acts and speech which are too public have, at root, a nuisance factor. Religion, we know, is not to be discussed in polite company – there is no quicker way to divide a room. As with the dinner table, so with the public square. Those who go about seeking to proselytise, even to evangelise, are at risk of contravening long-standing principles of non-interference: 'Live and let live', and 'I don't care if you're religious, as long as you don't push it on me'. They intrude on the day-to-day rubbing along of common life. People want to get on with their day, with their work or their shopping, without being preached at through megaphones for whatever cause.

In the second sense, the incivility of proselytism relates to the way in which it places the good of the proselytiser above the public good of those they seek to proselytise. Of course, this proselytising incivility might not be necessarily religious in nature. In spite of an illustrious history of social and political engagement amongst evangelicals, the word 'evangelical' is now probably less used to describe a theological position than the characteristic of being over-committed to something. We tend to feel that people who are 'evangelical' about whatever (veganism, cricket, a particular music group or a political campaign) are more interested in their cause than they are in you. You become the means of some other ideological, corporate or religious goal.

This will become particularly problematic if the group in question operates some kind of public function or provides some kind of public service.[3] They will, so the argument goes, subvert these services, using them to achieve their own religious objectives – an act of bad faith when spending the public pound. At this point, secularist campaigners argue, people are either put-off using a service with a strong faith identity for fear of being 'bible-bashed' or have to put-up with a service that they're unhappy with.

What is the result? When we come across those that fail to honour the requirements of civility, be they chuggers, political campaigners or aggressive salesmen, we are likely to cross to the other side of the metaphorical road, or perhaps look to public authorities to control these activities. When it comes to the religious proselytiser, the problem is all the more acute – faith speech is considered particularly 'uncivil' because of the significance and comprehensiveness of the convictions that religious people seek to share, and therefore the weight of the challenge which they offer to others. In some senses, a street preacher might be like 'chugger' but in this he is different: he or she might make us uncomfortable in ways that a 'chugger' never could. For Philip Howard, enjoining shoppers passing London's Oxford Circus not to be "sinners but winners", or calling them "shopaholic robots", this resulted in Westminster Council obtaining an Anti-Social Behaviour Order against him in 2006.

These complaints are not straw men to be knocked over. When 'in public' – in shared public spaces and performing public functions – people of good faith should speak and act in ways which make for the common good. In fact, one of the very good reasons to affirm a general aspiration for civility – and ordered public space – is the desire to have a society where profound claims can be spoken and heard. In a room where everyone is shouting no-one will be heard.

Two questions flow from this – in principle, is advocacy of one's religious views necessarily a form of incivility and, empirically, is the charge that FBOs prioritise their own objectives over the public good a fair one? We explore these below.

the liberal case for public faith

The issue of the general 'bother factor' of public religion is relatively easily dealt with.

In practice, most religious people accept the need for civility. For every Philip Howard there are many more people of faith cringing when they walk past a Philip Howard. But even when people really are irritating, that's not sufficient reason to try and silence them, particularly through coercive means. The legal philosopher Jeremy Waldron offers the following thought experiment:

> Imagine a society which is religiously homogeneous except for one small but highly active dissident sect. The existence of that sect is an irritant to the majority faith; it makes the majority feel uncomfortable... So a political proposal is made and defended on utilitarian grounds: the sect is to be banned from any further activity in the society; they will not be allowed to worship or proselytize.[4]

What, asks Waldron, has gone wrong here? The problem is that comfort and religious freedom are being weighed on the same scale, ignoring the *qualitative* difference between the two. The discomfort of the majority is of less significance than the significance of the right of the small sect to worship. For the same reason, it is important to protect broad freedoms to proselytise – it might well be annoying, but it's also very valuable. Unlike advertising, religious discussion challenges not just superficial beliefs (preferring this product to that), nor even

It is important to protect broad freedoms to proselytise – it might well be annoying, but it's also very valuable.

just strongly held personal commitments (being a member of this political party rather than that), but foundational assumptions about the good life and what it is to be human. On basic liberal principles, it is better that these are tested in open and honest debate.

It would be illustrative to explore this point in connection which the school environment, since this is perhaps the single field of public services where religious denominations and FBOs are most engaged. It is clear that, amongst all the different kinds of school with a religious and non-religious foundation, there is a huge variation of practice vis-à-vis religious education. In a recent report on religion and belief in schools, the academic Linda Woodhead and former Secretary of State for Education Charles Clarke distinguish between three different approaches that have been adopted in different times and places within religious studies: religious instruction/'indoctrination', formation and education.[5]

The first they treat as the business of worshipping faith communities alone, but the latter two can and should be part of what schools do. Even the least controversial of the three – religious education – would recognise diversity, encourage students to learn 'about' and 'from' religious and nonreligious worldviews, and would involve both 'understanding religions' and 'religious understanding'. In other words, it would involve being exposed to religious claims and counter claims, even if these are thought to be frustrating and objectionable.

From an educational perspective, it's clearly right that students should have a sense of what is 'out there' in the religious market place. Why shouldn't they, for instance, have copies of the *Young Atheist's Handbook* in their libraries (though we should dismiss rum claims that sending the books to secondary schools doesn't constitute a form of proselytising)?[6] Woodhead and Clarke argue that students should be supported to develop the ability to articulate and develop their own values and commitments, and the capacity to debate and engage with others.

On a general level, the point is first that proselytism may be irritating but it is important and, second, that being able to share one's faith, and presumably having a thick enough skin to accept it when others do the same – is constitutive of the public good. In a room where everyone is shouting, no-one can be heard – but in a room where no-one says anything, no-one is heard either. Rather than being the betrayal of civility, coherently articulating and defending fundamental religious beliefs is one of its most important foundations.

faith, hope and love, or money, influence and power?

The second part of the complaint is more difficult to deal with. Here it is asserted that when FBOs are in receipt of *public* funds, they are acting on behalf of the state. Like the state they are mandated to prioritise the public good. But isn't it the case that when a public service is being delivered by a religious provider there will necessarily be some other motivation, even if subtly hidden? An analogy could be drawn with public service reforms which include for-profit providers – isn't the public service ethos compromised by a profit motive? In the same way, the integrity of a service might be compromised by evangelistic religious agendas. *Ipso facto…*

In fact, we would contest the premise. Faith-based charities should, by their own lights, work to reach members of the community who do not necessarily share their faith, or even those who may share their faith but feel in other ways that they might be discriminated against (e.g., the LGBTQ community). In other words, they are to serve the common good, but that is not because they have been funded by the state – they are, state funded or not, under an obligation to serve the common good, and many things that promote the common good have nothing to do with the state. Public funding of such activities is the state acting to support the work of independent providers, not to turn them into its own organs or representatives. The state doesn't support FBOs because they can deliver public goods, but because they already do and already should.

From an arch-secular perspective, though, religious institutions want power, control, money and influence, and the route to those things is more people in the pews. In our interviews, even among those that are broadly positive about working with religious organisations and FBOs, there was a lingering suspicion around the double motivation of FBOs. One statutory sector interviewee said to us:

> *From an arch-secular perspective, though, religious institutions want power, control, money and influence.*

> It's about putting aside your private gain – you know, "what's in it for me?" – and separating your own agenda from the needs of another person. The issue is, is this in their public interests, and not in your private gain – there [should be] nothing in it that benefits you.

Of course, just as there may be other people who are selfishly motivated, there may be some religious institutions or individuals who do have private gains in mind. There are, however, very many more who are motivated by a vision for the common good. As the

CEO of a large homelessness charity put it to us, quoting directly from the Bible, "The only thing that counts is faith expressing itself through love". In other words – faith must be expressed in acts of service.

There is need also for FBOs to be absolutely explicit about what they're trying do.

Civility does not require FBOs to secularise for the sake of public participation, but to identify their own reasons for seeking the good of their community, including the religious other, in all aspects. This is not to argue for a free-for-all for whatever agenda people want to pursue by whatever means. Being rooted in the kind of holistic, generous and other-oriented religious mission, even when it includes explicit evangelism, doesn't undervalue or ignore the 'public' interests of the other.

There is need also for FBOs to be absolutely explicit about what they're trying do, leaving no room for accusations of duplicity or dishonesty. The CEO of a Christian debt advice agency emphasised to us how important this already was to them:

> We're very open about the fact that we want to see people's lives transformed… We do have guidelines for what we see as appropriate in a setting of where you're delivering social care… some things are just more appropriate for a church context. That's partly about respecting individuals, partly it's around recognising that when people are new to faith or just exploring faith then there are some things which should be off limits.

in summary

This chapter acknowledges that in a 'secular' society, religious evangelism will frequently prove frustrating. We acknowledge too that there will be fears that the religious are motivated by something other than serving the common good. The characterisation of religious mission as necessarily or fundamentally self-serving – that, in other words, public religion is a form of incivility – is a mistaken one. The same interviewee mentioned above said, "they think that we are out to get something, but we're not trying to get anything from anyone, we're trying to give something away".

Ultimately, the issue is one which is open to empirical observation. Where are the FBOs that proselytise in the sense meant by religion's critics? There is, it must be said, scant evidence for claims that faith-based services disingenuously use their position to proselytise, preference their own faith community, or are off-putting to secular or minority religious users.[7] On the contrary, our own research suggests that many vulnerable people find state services highly conditional, while faith-based interventions are seen as having greater concern for the dignity of the service user.[8]

Tellingly, none of the statutory interviewees were able to report actual historic examples of occasions when, for example, faith agencies had misspent public funding for the purposes of proselytization – "In all the time [I've been here] I've not come across any serious examples… It's more a perception of what could happen". If nothing else, then we must also recall that all commissioned public service providers operate under some of the most stringent equality legislation in the world.

It would seem that the problem in theory is greater than the problem in practice, and that FBOs accept the conditions of public engagement. Indeed, if FBOs ought to do something different, it would be to be more confident and more explicit when it comes to their ethos, aims, objectives and ways of working. There is no reason to assume that this should compromise their ability to serve the public good.

chapter 2 – references

1   Peter Berger, *The Sacred Canopy: Elements of a Sociological Theory of Religion* (Anchor, 1967), p. 138.

2   Edward Shils "The Virtue of Civil Society," *Government and Opposition* 26.1 (1991), p. 11. Cited in Derek Edyvane, "The Passion for Civility". Forthcoming in *Political Studies Review*.

3   Following John Rawls in *Political Liberalism* (Columbia University Press, 1996), p. 224, civility is "to be able to explain to one another on those fundamental questions how the principles and policies they advocate and vote for can be supported by the political values of public reason". Political philosophers will be quick to note that Rawls never intended for such a criteria to be applied to all public speech, but only to the speech of individuals performing a public function. Yet that is partly what is at issue when religious organisations, with strong and distinctive conceptions of 'the good', take on a public function.

4   Jeremy Waldron, *The Law* (Routledge, 1990), p. 106. Waldron offers the case to illustrate the limitations of utilitarian calculus in the making of law, but the parable makes our point perfectly.

5   Linda Woodhead and Charles Clarke, *A New Settlement: Religion and Belief in Schools* (Westminster Faith Debates, 2015), p. 33. Available at http://faithdebates.org.uk/wp-content/uploads/2015/06/A-New-Settlement-for-Religion-and-Belief-in-schools.pdf (accessed 19.08.2015).

6   "Humanists put faith to test by giving schools free copies of atheist 'bible'", *The Independent*, 29 April 2013. Available at http://www.independent.co.uk/news/education/education-news/humanists-put-faith-to-test-by-giving-schools-free-copies-of-atheist-bible-9303706.html (accessed 19.08.2013).

7   For instance, Johnsen's study (cited above) even found that users are rarely aware that the service they are using is delivered by an FBO.

8   See, for instance, Paul Bickley, *Good Neighbours: How Churches Help Communities Flourish* (Theos/Church Urban Fund, 2014). Available at https://www.cuf.org.uk/sites/default/files/PDFs/Research/Good%20Neighbours%20Report-CUF-Theos-2014.pdf (accessed 19.08.2015).

proselytism in multicultural societies

So far, we have argued that the word proselytism is unclear in meaning, simply describing a range of religious things we disapprove of. Accusations that religious organisations will use public position or public money to proselytise are a campaigning tactic used to block faith-based service providers from greater engagement.

In the previous section, we have seen how proselytism could be understood as a form of 'incivility'. We have suggested both that 'civility' actually requires that people are able to coherently articulate their convictions, and observed how religious organisations do not act in bad faith. For instance, they are – and should be – honest and explicit about their intentions, so that potential partners and even service users 'know where they stand'.

If the complaint from incivility relates to how religious people and institutions act 'in public', there might also be concerns about how proselytising religions can coexist. It is to this issue that we now turn.

the fact of religious diversity

Increased religious diversity in the UK is well documented, a local outcome of both larger processes of migration and demographic change.

From the Western European perspective, this looks mainly like a process of secularisation. The most marked change in the UK over recent decades has been the growth in the number of people who have no religious affiliation or religious belief, alongside a marked reduction in the number of people that identify with 'mainline' Christian denominations. The largest single group is now those with no religion – 49 per cent, up from 31 per cent in 1983 (though this should not necessarily be taken to mean that the religious 'nones' are convinced or ardent metaphysical materialists[1]). By way of contrast, in 1983 40 per cent of respondents to the British Social Attitudes survey said that they were Anglican. In 2014, the corresponding figure was 17 per cent. All Christian denominations taken together make up 42 per cent of the population, and – contrary to public perception – around five per cent of respondents are Muslim.[2]

This is, of course, almost the opposite of international trends, where the proportion of the global population that don't affiliate to any religion is shrinking, whereas Islam continues to grow and Christianity remains stable. At both the national and international level, therefore, there is a perceived need to regulate the often tense interactions of religious traditions. In particular, adherents to traditions or belief systems that are shrinking might suggest, with some justification, that Islam and Christianity in particular can come not just as beliefs alongside many others, but as part of overweening cultural and political systems – cultural imperialism, for want of a better phrase. Makua Matua, a human rights scholar and Professor of Law at Buffalo Law School, finds that the impact of Christianity and Islam in Africa has been disastrous, undermining indigenous religions and practices like traditional healing and polygamy. Christianity and Islam have come "not as guests but masters", and left behind people who "are neither African nor European nor Arab".[3]

> There is a perceived need to regulate the often tense interactions of religious traditions.

The point is made most strongly in regard to indigenous peoples who, so the argument goes, are especially in need of protection from a kind of cultural vandalism where art, language and customs are swept aside along with religious beliefs. In the UK, however, a similar case has been made by those from minority and non-proselytising faith traditions. Such traditions value religious pluralism, which moves beyond the mere recognition of diversity to the active advocacy of it, and a philosophical claim that all religious traditions have a similar truth value – are 'equally valid'. Consider this from Jay Lakhani, the education director of the Hindu Council UK.

> Every religion is entitled to make claims about its pathway and promote it to its adherents, but when it attempts to impose its pathway on people of other faiths or no faith, a religion can turn into an explosive device… One casualty of pluralism would be the proselytising agendas of missionary religions. I suspect this is the real reason why there is such resistance to this simple but potent concept.[4]

is religion the same as culture?

These are legitimate concerns and should not be lightly dismissed. The difficulty here is that religious identities and cultural, social and political ideas and identities are not wholly distinct from each other. It is not so much the advocacy of religious beliefs, but the advocacy of social mores or ideas which are closely associated with that belief which might adversely affect other groups, and not just other religious groups, which becomes a source of concern. An officer in a local authority told us about some of his institution's "red lines" around working with faith groups:

> … as a local authority there are some things that we do expect from a publicly funded body. The obvious one which I'm sure you're aware of is the perceived clash between religion and belief and gender and sexual orientation equality… The law is really clear. Religions are free to practice tenets of their faith which might involve not allowing women in certain positions of authority, might not accept certain sexual orientation minorities etc. in terms of the practicing of their faith in a religious context. However, that can't transcribe into any provision of a service to the public. That's really straight-forward.

Though they are not the subject of this report, employment tribunals involving questions of religion and belief do not relate so much to some irreducible core religious doctrine so much as their social expression, particularly with regard to sexual orientation.[5] It is noteworthy that in the 'Trojan Horse' scandal, where state schools in Muslim majority areas of Birmingham were reportedly co-opted by those seeking to expound a conservative strain of Islam, most of the concerns raised were about teaching or practice on social and political issues, including around gender equality and views on the state of Israel.[6]

Most of the concerns raised were about teaching or practice on social and political issues.

It would be wrong to attempt to create too great a distinction between religious beliefs and religious practices and mores.[7] All religious and non-religious positions have a view of 'the good life' and how society might be arranged to allow for it to be lived – these are not incidental extras to religious doctrines. Ethics, of course, is rooted in metaphysics. At the same time, religions emerge from particular cultures, and are practiced in particular cultures – they influence these cultures and are influenced by them. It is, however, mistaken to suggest that religions never transcend their culture.

Religious proselytism will to a greater or lesser extent, depending on the religion in question, involve claims about how people should live (though many ethical, political, and social questions are also matters of contention with in religions). Ultimately, however, the sharing of faith is not only that – it doesn't necessarily devalue the way of life of the religious or ethnic other.

Equally, there are far too many historical instances where religion has come as part of an imperialist package – people will point to the cultural imperialism of Christian empires in the 18th and 19th centuries. As Elmer Thiessen notes, even during periods of the worst colonial imperialism, as with the Spanish conquest of the central Americas, there are instances where the missionary religion has sought to protect indigenous communities.[8]

From a contemporary Christian perspective, part of the task of mission is to correlate the universal gospel with the particular culture and context with which it has come into contact. The implicit vision of the relationship between religion and culture is not just that Christianity *can* transcend the cultural assumptions of its advocates, but that it *should* transcend them. This is more than a point of evangelistic technique, it is the nature of the gospel. The missionary may indeed 'go native', inhabiting, valuing and collaborating in the preservation of the culture in question even if in part it offers a critique and tension.

In the UK context, this might become a question of how FBOs relate to service users who do not identify with the charity's faith or ethos. Those we spoke to, whether in receipt of public money or not, were eager to point out that they do not discriminate on the grounds of religion or belief (or sexual orientation, for that matter). One put it to us that, "We want people to have an experience of inclusion... The way we are best able to export the Christian message is by an experience of inclusion, in particular when a lot of our [service users] start a long way back". Another interviewee, a chaplain, said that he didn't want to make the people he sought to serve "like me" – he did not want to make them believe and behave as he did.

Religious belief motivates people in complex ways, at least as much to hospitality and inclusivity.

However, this did not necessarily mean that they took a low key approach when it came to the ethos. Strong religious belief motivates people in complex ways, at least as much to hospitality and inclusivity as to a desire to spread a religious message. Even very explicitly religious acts might not be intended to convert, or even attract, new adherents from other religious backgrounds. Another interviewee, a charity worker working with a (non-publicly funded) Christian FBO, explained to us how they would offer to pray for clients, even if they identified as belonging to another religion.

> At the end of a visit with a client I will normally say, "you know we're from a Christian agency. I would like to offer prayer for you – if you would like it. You don't have to have it, it's not something that will affect how we treat you, if you say no then that's fine... but if you would like I would love to pray for you". I always explain that I will pray in the name of Jesus, because we have a lot of Muslim clients, and Hindu and Sikh. The people that turn me down tend to be ex-Catholics. The Muslims, the Hindus, the Sikhs love it that we pray for them.

Affirming the dignity and integrity of ethnic and religious groups, and their cultures and practices, does not necessitate a full-blown multi-faithism or religious relativism. Indeed, as Jonathan Chaplin has argued in *Multiculturalism: A Christian Retrieval*, "suppression of religious differences is a recipe not for tolerance but for mutual disrespect".[9] There is a necessary work of ongoing critique, both of our own practices and those of others, and "only naïve cultural relativists or religious pluralists will pretend it can be circumvented".[10] Some of the FBO leaders we spoke to argued that it was – paradoxically – a lack of confidence and clarity around a theological identity they would result in it being articulated in more shrill and brittle ways. As the CEO of a large FBO put it:

> If you're not clear how you understand God or your theology, or you're not capable of articulating that in a way that facilitates inclusion, then you'll end up being something different to what you say you are.

In some cases, chaplaincy is a model of engagement which can incorporates just such a model of pastoral and spiritual care for all faiths and none regardless of the religious identity of the chaplain. One chaplain explained, "The individual is there to meet the faith needs of his or her own, but [also to] facilitate the needs of others. I'm not a Muslim, but I'll find you one. I'm not a Baptist, but I'll find you one".

religious freedom, religious protectionism

Nevertheless, it has to be acknowledged that not all groups are equal. We are bound to ask, what are the prevailing cultural norms and what impositions do they make on religious minorities? At this point our discussion of proselytism connects directly to religious freedom. On the face of it, the legal protection of religious freedoms is the most obvious way to ensure that religious beliefs aren't trampled on. However, the rightful desire to protect religious or other minorities can too easily be used as an excuse for religious protectionism.

The freedom to convert is clearly set out in various international rights charters, treaties and covenants (including, as above, in Article 9 of the European Convention on Human Rights). Article 18 of the International Covenant on Civil and Political Rights, which affirms one's right to "manifest (one's) religion or belief in worship, observance, practice and teaching". The only caveat to this right is the rather vague – and broad – caution which follows.

> Freedom to manifest one's religion or beliefs may be subject only to such limitations as are prescribed by law and are necessary to protect public safety, order, health, or morals or the fundamental rights and freedoms of others.

A relatively small percentage of the world's population live with no restrictions on the manifestation of their religious belief.

While it may be the case that most states are signatory to these conventions, these hazy grounds for limitation are subject to broad interpretation and stand behind a wide range of restrictions placed on this 'freedom to manifest' under national legislation. In 2013, Pew Forum found that 42 countries across the globe have some degree of government-enforced limitation specifically focused on proselytism, amongst 59 countries whose governments had some kind of restriction on religious belief or practice.[11] A relatively small percentage of the world's population live with no restrictions on the manifestation of their religious belief.

This is a particular problem across the Muslim world. Since Sharia expressly forbids apostasy and blasphemy, the extent to which 'Muslim countries' restrict proselytism often reflects the extent to which it has been incorporated into public governance. For example, Algeria protects the right to freedom of non-Muslim religion, but religious practices must not violate public order, morality, or the rights of others. Ordinance 06-03, issued in 2006, is the practical outworking of this principle; it lists proselytising (or even an act which might "shake the faith of a Muslim") by non-Muslims as a criminal offence, carrying a maximum punishment of one million dinars ($12,816 at today's exchange rate) and five years' imprisonment. In this instance, someone guilty of 'proselytism' is one who "incites, constrains, or utilizes means of seduction tending to convert a Muslim to another religion; or by using to this end establishments of teaching, education, health, social, culture, training...or any financial means."[12]

Such legislation casts the religious majority as vulnerable and in need of protection. Similar strictures apply across most of the Muslim world and, of course, in some jurisdictions carry a death sentence. The most notorious prosecutions tend to involve either western Christian missionaries or Christians native to those jurisdictions, but other traditions – including atheism and minority Muslim sects (e.g., Ahmadis) – suffer from discrimination.

However, it is important to note that non-Muslim cultures also often seek to prohibit or control proselytism. Though constitutionally secular, Russia also recognises the "special contribution" made by Russian Orthodoxy to the history and culture of the country, which, in practice, translates into special privileges and protections for the religion against infringement by other religious groups. The Russian Orthodox Church is anxious that its 'canonical territory' is not infringed upon by other Christian denominations, leading to infamously tense relations with the Roman Catholic Church. It has therefore allied itself closely with the Russian state, resulting in an ethno-religious essentialism which squeezes religious and non-religious traditions in the name of a secure national identity.

Additional laws banning "extremism" and "offending the religious feelings of believers" provide room for broader proselytism convictions, and, according to the US International Religious Freedom Report, pose a particular threat to minority religious groups – those who worship outside of the four 'traditional' faiths of Russia (Orthodox Christianity, Islam, Judaism and Buddhism).

India is, again, a secular republic, notionally giving all religions equality under the law. However, the majority status of Hinduism, as well as the prominence of Hindu nationalist ministers in government and the power of state and local government and law enforcement means that legislation surrounding proselytism tends to operate differently depending on the state and its balance of religious groups. The US International Religious Freedom Report pointed to some state governments enforcing anti-conversion laws, and local police and enforcement agencies failing to respond to attacks against religious witness from minority groups. The All India Christian Council reported that in 2013 Christian preachers and missionaries in Andhra Pradesh were subject to 46 uninvestigated incidents of harassment and/or physical intimidation in July of that year, while a legal challenge from Jehovah's Witnesses (who, in 2000, were stopped from receiving foreign contributions as they posed a "serious threat to the public peace and tranquility") remained pending. Hindu nationalist organisations claimed that Christian missionaries were making 'rice-Christians' of low-caste Hindus, while Christians responded that among Hindu groups the 're-converting' of these new Christians was also carried out fraudulently.[13]

Even liberal-secular states look to control proselytism – indeed, their construction of liberalism and, again, national identity itself is explicitly built around controls on public religious expression. French laïcité enforces particular codes of state-defined secular behaviour in areas considered to be the 'public square'. In popular consciousness this is most closely associated with the ban on religious symbols in schools in 2004, a law described by the then Assembly Speaker as a "clear affirmation that public school is a place for learning and not for militant activity or proselytism."[14] As such, when the case of a Sikh boy who had been expelled from school for wearing a keski was taken to the Human Rights Committee of the UN Convention on Civil and Political Rights in 2008, the complainant emphasised that the concept of proselytism was foreign to the Sikh religion, that the Sikh community was in no way involved in proselytism in the French community at large, and, as such, his keski could in no way be considered an act of proselytism.[15] The distinction between religious traditions which explicitly include religious witness and those which do not does not appear to have an impact on French rulings concerning their manifestation in the public square, suggesting that 'proselytism' is, in this instance, being used to refer to a much broader form of public influence. The presence of any kind of religious conviction or symbol, whether it is explicitly intended to attract or recruit new adherents or not, threatens laïcité.

In each instance here, and in others that could be explored, religious freedom is curtailed because other religions are seen as threatening foreign influences, undermining fundamental assumptions about who 'we' are. Proselytism is an action of subversion, challenging articulations of national and religious identity, even in purportedly liberal states. To be French is to be secular, to be Moroccan is to be Muslim, to be Russian is to be Russian Orthodox… a twenty-first century kind of *cuius regio, eius religio*.[16]

proselytism and British values

This may be an interesting tour of different states' approaches to religious diversity, and their willingness or otherwise to protect religious liberties, but is this of any practical relevance in the UK?

In the British context, religious diversity has until recently been managed with a light touch under the rubric of 'multiculturalism'. This doctrine, of course, has fallen on hard times. The rapidity and patterns of religious changes have resulted in new stresses and pressures on public services (as seen in the so-called Trojan Horse scandal). In the last decade or so, governments have recently become more interventionist, seeking to legislatively manage this 'superdiversity' (e.g., the Racial and Religious Hatred Act 2006 and the Equality Act 2010). Some of these measures have had direct bearing on questions around proselytism. Following a campaign involving both religious and non-religious critics, the Racial and Religious Hatred Bill was amended with a declamatory clause clarifying that the Act should not be "read or given effect in a way which prohibits or restricts…proselytising or urging adherents of a different religion or belief system to cease practising their religion or belief system".[17] The Coalition Government, and now the Conservative administration, have continued down this more interventionist route. Most notably, they have mandated schools to promote democracy, the rule of law, individual liberty and mutual respect and tolerance of those with different faiths and beliefs as 'British values'.

> *These 'values' are treated as essential rather than procedural – about 'who we are', rather than about 'how we do things'.*

No-one would pretend that the problems the government is trying to resolve through the introduction of a requirement to teach British values are easily solved, but the agenda has clear implications for how schools with a religious character express their religious ethos – arguably, the policy would be completely ineffective if it did not. Nor are the values 'wrong'. The problem is rather that these 'values' are treated as essential rather than procedural – about 'who we are', rather than about 'how we do things'. This can't but set up a tension between religious and other identities, one where proselytising for certain faiths or views becomes not only objectionable but subversive though, as we have discussed, the focus is not usually on religious views in the sense of metaphysical beliefs, but on their social, ethical and political implications. And what will we do about an idea or tradition that is defined as un-British?

Interviewees from FBOs objected to what one described as the 'myth of neutrality' - that they were cast as they agencies with and ethos, identity and agenda, singling them out for particular oversight. If one of the problems of proselytism is that it threatens minorities, then focusing on the way religious traditions might intrude on the culture, practices and norms of others looks arbitrary to FBOs. In countries like France, and increasingly the United Kingdom, it is not the religious other that seeks to change or challenge minority cultures, but the principles of *laïcité* or 'British values'. The state which controls religious proselytism may well have one eye on the protection of the identity, practice and customs of religious minorities, but the other is on defending its own most essential presumptions.

in summary

In this chapter we have argued that one of the concerns about religious proselytism is that it threatens the security and integrity of minority religious groups, or indeed other minority identities. Religion is deeply bound with culture, and that to advocate for a religious tradition is often to argue for distinctive and often highly contentious social, political or moral ideas. However, some religious traditions can and do transcend their cultural sources, so that they can become genuinely 'contextual' examples of that tradition.

We have described a global trend in religious 'protectionism' which, though often defending controls of proselytism on the basis of protecting religious minorities, tends to assure the position of religious majorities or indeed a non-faith position. We have posed a question – does the 'British values' agenda represent just such an example?

Arguably, the religious need to pay greater attention to understanding and articulating the relationship between their faith and the kinds of social, political and ethical views which they advocate, and show greater understanding of the way these impinge on the freedoms of other religious traditions or social minorities. That said, it is hard to see how controlling religious expression – suppressing religious difference, as Jonathan Chaplin puts it – will ultimately deliver the kind of society we want to live in. The choice is between combining freedom and self-discipline in religious public action, or combining indiscipline with a lack of freedom.

chapter 3 – references

1   Many of those people who deliberately place themselves outside the boundary of any formal religious belief or adherence – by calling themselves an atheist, or saying that they belong to no religion, or never participating in a religious service as a worshipper – have some Christian and/or spiritual beliefs and, on occasion, even practices. See Nick Spencer and Holly Weldin, *Post-religious Britain?: The Faith of the Faithless* (Theos, 2012).

2   NatCen Social Research, "British Social Attitudes: Church of England decline has accelerated in past decade". Available at http://www.natcen.ac.uk/news-media/press-releases/2015/may/british-social-attitudes-church-of-england-decline-has-accelerated-in-past-decade/ (accessed 19.08.2014).

3   Quoted in Grace Y. Kao, "The Logic of Anti-Proselytization, Revisited", in Rosalind I.J. Hackett ed., *Proselytization Revisited: Rights Talk, Free Markets and Culture Wars* (Routledge, 2008), p. 88.

4   "All faiths must accept pluralism if we are to defuse strife caused in the name of religion", *The Guardian*, 3 November 2007. Available at http://www.theguardian.com/commentisfree/2007/nov/03/comment.religion (accessed 19.08.2015).

5   "Christian nursery worker sacked over anti-gay views wins tribunal case", *The Guardian*, 7 June 2015. Available at http://www.theguardian.com/law/2015/jun/07/christian-nursery-worker-sacked-over-anti-gay-views-wins-tribunal-case (accessed 17.09.15).

6   "Trojan Horse 'plot' schools timeline", BBC News Online, 16 July 2015. Available at http://www.bbc.co.uk/news/uk-england-birmingham-28370552 (accessed 19.08.2015).

7   For a useful and succinct exploration of the question, see Jonathan Chaplin, *Multiculturalism: A Christian Retrieval* (Theos, 2011), pp. 56-58.

8   Thiessen, *Ethics of Evangelism*, p. 100.

9   Chaplin, *Multiculturalism*, p. 52.

10   Chaplin, *Multiculturalism*, p. 53.

11   Pew Research Centre, *Latest Trends in Religious Restrictions and Hostilities* (2015). Available at http://www.pewforum.org/files/2015/02/Restrictions2015_fullReport.pdf (accessed 19.08.2015).

12   Bureau of Democracy, Human Rights and Labor, 2013 *International Religious Freedom Report*, 2014, United States Department of State. Available at http://www.state.gov/j/drl/rls/irf/2013/nea/222283.htm (accessed 19.08.2015).

13   International Religious Freedom Report (2013). Available at http://www.state.gov/j/drl/rls/irf/2013/sca/222329.htm (accessed 19.08.2015).

14   "French MPs Vote to Ban Headscarves", Sky News, 10 February 2004. Available at http://news.sky.com/story/245721/french-mps-vote-to-ban-headscarves (accessed 19.08.2015)

15   Judgement is available at http://unitedsikhs.org/rtt/doc/BikramjitSinghDecision.pdf (accessed 18.08.2015).

16   A Latin phrase meaning "Whose realm, his religion".

17   Clause 29J, Racial and Religious Hatred Act, 2006. See http://www.legislation.gov.uk/ukpga/2006/1/contents (accessed 16.09.2015).

proselytism and vulnerability

In previous chapters, we have set out the difficulty of offering a clear and meaningful description of proselytism, and described two critiques of proselytism – that it represents a form of incivility, and that it threatens religious and social minorities. In response, we have argued that civility actually requires that we are capable of articulating our beliefs to others and that religious traditions are capable of respecting minority practices and cultures. Indeed, that religious minorities have dignity and deserve sensitive treatment is one reason why proselytism should not be heavily circumscribed.

In this chapter, we turn to the issues around coercion, power and vulnerability. As in previous chapters, we concede that these issues present clear challenges for religious witness, not least when it comes to the practice of FBOs. However, we will argue that we should be careful not to 'vulnerable-ise' service users, assuming that religion should be kept off the table, and failing therefore to address spiritual needs even in ways that are strongly led by the service user (though clearly in some contexts greater care might be required).

the 'faith sector': increasing demand, increasing supply

> The lady handed out the tea, and while we ate and drank she moved to and fro, talking benignly. She talked upon religious subjects—about Jesus Christ always having a soft spot for poor rough men like us, and about how quickly the time passed when you were in church, and what a difference it made to a man on the road if he said his prayers regularly. We hated it.

In *Down and Out in Paris and London*, George Orwell paints a vivid picture of what it was like in to be reliant on the 'charity' of the religious in the inter-war period. It was not charity at all but an exchange. "'You 'ad your bun,' said another; 'you got to pay for it.' 'Pray for it, you mean. Ah, you don't get much for nothing.'"[1] These stories stick long in the memory and, as welfare spending is subjected to downward pressures, cause us to wonder – are we going back there?

In her recently updated *Religion in Britain: A Persistent Paradox*, sociologist Grace Davie asks "why...has there been growth rather than decline in the presence of faith communities in the welfare provision of a modern western democracy, which is becoming more rather than less secular?"[2] For Davie, it is clear that there is both a shortage of money and an increase in demand when it comes to state-based welfare services. These trends began to emerge in the 1970s following the oil crisis, and the 2008 recession simply made a tricky situation more difficult. A demand therefore arose for other actors to deliver the services previously provided directly by the state. The agenda has unfolded at the level of political narrative (i.e., the Big Society), social policy and public funding, with the question of the appropriateness or otherwise of faith-based providers becoming part of that wider agenda. Inevitably, some have been warmly supportive of FBOs, while others – including some religious voices – have expressed concerns.

What has been less well observed is an increase in the supply of FBOs, ranging from the local worshipping congregations to large-scale providers with a faith ethos. At the local level, religious congregations are motivated to devote more of their time, energy, money and attention into social projects. The recent Cinnamon Network Faith Action Audits, based on a survey of faith

> *Religious congregations are motivated to devote more of their time, energy, money and attention into social projects.*

groups in 57 towns across the UK, extrapolated from their findings that faith groups nationally could be delivering 220,000 social action projects, serving up to 48 million beneficiaries and mobilising 2 million volunteers. The large majority of this activity is privately funded charitable action, but these 'audits' are the latest in a long list, all of which point to the substantial appetite for charitable endeavour in religious organisations.[3]

Davie rightly notes that the welfare state never wholly displaced the social role of churches and other faith institutions.[4] Now, at a national level, the 'Third Sector' has been invited to participate in the transformation of public services, where a diverse range of providers are engaged in key public services (e.g., the operation of academy schools, probation services or the DWP work programme). When it comes to faith-based charities, increased religious diversity, cultural discomfort with religious belief, alongside the ways in which religious traditions are mandated to love their neighbour, mean that faith organisations are increasingly finding their public legitimacy through serving those in need.

Needless to say, one of the key concerns raised by critics has been the potential of groups taking advantage of the opportunity to proselytise: "services may become 'balkanised' on the grounds of religion or belief which will be both uneconomical and divisive.

Organisations may also use their status as service providers to proselytise". Even the Salvation Army, a highly regarded denomination and national charity with a long tradition of faith-based social action has been accused of dubious intent:

> ...the Salvation Army is 'to proclaim his gospel, to persuade people of all ages to become his disciples and to engage in a programme of practical concern for the needs of humanity.' Such an agenda is not compatible with state provision of public services...[5]

Central to these anxieties is the view that when a religious agency performs such a function it is in a position of power over vulnerable people. As Jack London put in *The People of the Abyss*, "it is the way of the world that when one man feeds another he is that man's master".

proselytism and power

In the case of *Larissis and Others v Greece* (1998), the European Court of Human Rights considered the conviction of several officers in the Greek Air Force for proselytism. The applicants (the officers) were members of a Pentecostal Church, and their conviction concerned proselytising activities against members of the public and subordinates in the Air Force. As established in the case *Kokkinakis v. Greece* (1993), also concerning a conviction for proselytism in Greece, the court was clear that the conviction constituted an interference with Article 9 rights. The question in this instance was whether the restrictions were necessary to protect the rights and interests of others.

The court found that the convictions in relation to the civilians were not justified. However, the court upheld the convictions in relation to the subordinate airmen.

> ... the hierarchical structures which are a feature of life in the armed forces may colour every aspect of the relations between military personnel, making it difficult for the subordinate to rebuff the approaches of an individual of superior rank or withdraw from a conversation initiated by him.[6]

In other words, the Court discerned a different application of the principle of free exercise when the question of relative power and vulnerability came into play. Their finding has a common sense value. Surely there will always be those who might take advantage of their influence to 'compel them to come in', as Augustine said of the Donatists.[7]

Vulnerability here could be multi-faceted. Anyone who is at an informational, financial or physical disadvantage or anyone who is dependent and therefore particularly open to physical, psychological or social coercion could be considered vulnerable. The theologian Grace Kao describes a number of instances where the tactics and targets of proselytising organisations have been called into question in the field of international aid and development.[8] The Islamic Defender's Front and Laskar Mujahidin brought aid in the wake of the 2004 Boxing Day Tsunami, along with an intention to preach Sharia and make new converts. WorldHelp – an evangelical development charity – sought to place 300 orphaned Muslim children from the Indonesian province of Banda Aceh into a Christian orphanage in Jakarta, with a view to planting Christian principles and returning them to the region when grown to reach others (after some outrage in Indonesia, WorldHelp abandoned the plan). As Kao puts it, no wonder critics view the combination of preaching with aid with grave misgivings and even contempt.

In the domestic context, we do not tend to see such extreme need. Nevertheless, could it be the case that, even unintentionally, churches and faith-based organisations providing services to the public might seem to oblige service users to accept invitations to attend worship services or social events or accept offers of prayer?[9] One of our interviewees, albeit someone specifically working on engaging FBOs in service provision, highlighted the issue of client vulnerability. She argued, from previous experience as a counsellor, that vulnerable people were "porous" and might not be making "good, objective decisions", and

> *Couldn't any religious social action be described as a kind of a bribe?*

that, often unintentionally, religious institutions have a kind of "gravitational pull". Even in its most inoffensive form, couldn't any religious social action be described as a kind of a bribe? As St Francis of Assisi probably didn't say, "preach the Gospel; if necessary, use words".

Some may believe that such charges are rooted in anti-religious prejudice. There may be an element of arbitrariness about them – most governments, for instance, approach international aid with some element of conditionality. Domestically, many state and third sector institutions look for behaviour change as part of the terms of a formal or informal contract to support the service user.

That said, there can be almost no justification for making the provision of support conditional on religious change in publicly funded services – and again, there is little evidence that FBOs do so. However, those that combine a strong missional motivation with the purpose of providing public services are in risky territory. There is no escaping imbalances in resources, wealth or power. The question is, is there a need or a duty for religious groups to go further, deliberately scrubbing their language and interactions, for fear of having even an unintentional influence – effectively fully secularising in case they break the trust of service users, or funders? The interviewee mentioned above thought so, and argued that FBOs needed capacity building support with training for volunteers, so that the service on offer was as accessible as possible to users.

> I know people don't like the word secularise, but I definitely think you need to mainstream your dialogue and your approach, not what you would practice in private with other believers, laying on hands or praying with people... If that's not for you, then don't serve general public people with public money. Go and do what you want to do, which is to extend your faith to other people who know that that's what you're doing.

vulnerable or vulnerable-ised?

Not withstanding some of the caveats set out already in this report – e.g., that faith-based organisations should be conscious of the public purposes of their engagement, particularly when publicly funded – an approach which effectively obliges FBOs not just to professionalise, but to secularise – ought to be questioned. Doesn't this undermine the very rationale of engaging FBOs in the first place? Why would we bother, if they were to behave and speak just as any other kind of organisation?

When exploring the issue of service user vulnerability, interviews with agencies demonstrated something of the gap between FBO understanding and that of commissioners or statutory providers. FBOs who wanted to weave their faith into the service they provided offered two relevant arguments.

Religious components of the service on offer were voluntary and optional.

First, they suggested that religious components of the service on offer were voluntary and optional – in other words, they would not seek to impose any religious influence. One interviewee, who was both involved in the leadership of a national charity and 'kept a hand in' at the local level, accepted that people had a set of expectations when they found out that the service was Christian (e.g., that they might have to go to church), but argued that this could be mitigated by assurances that the service was not conditional on the acceptance of offers of prayer, invitations to services, etc. He noted that, in his experience, "people were extremely happy to say no" to such offers. In other words, they had a sense of agency in the process. Vulnerability was therefore not weighed in the same way.

> About the vulnerability issue – I don't know quite what people think we're trying to do... They think that we are out to get something, but we're not trying to get anything off anyone, we're trying to give something away.

Second, interviewees felt that they had a holistic understanding of people's needs, which begged some engagement on a spiritual level. One a manager for a Christian drug treatment agency, made the point about the complexity of addiction – it could not be understood reductively as either a physical, social or psychological problem, and argued that a multifaceted problem needed a multifaceted solution. In a field like addiction, exploring ideas like forgiveness was key.

> Faith is core, it really is core. Our corporate understanding of addiction is bio-psycho-socio-spiritual model. Someone from the NTA [National Treatment Agency], not a Christian at all, described addiction as self-will run riot or a disease or a disorder of the will… we would see addressing the spiritual side of it is really important. Most of our guys are through detox in three weeks, but that's only the beginning of addressing the problem.

There is a risk that we treat service users as passive recipients.

The issue here is, who are 'the vulnerable' and are we sure, or have we assumed, that they lack a sense of spiritual agency because they are materially in need? There is a risk that we treat service users as passive recipients of whatever 'we' – that is, those with resources, wealth and power – choose to force on them. On the contrary, they may have strong religious beliefs of their own, which are not to be shifted by mere whim. In other words, 'service-users' are human beings – part of recognising their dignity involves encouraging their agency.

in summary

One of the factors driving concern about proselytism is the increased demand for and supply of FBOs who will 'take up the slack' when it comes to delivering public services. Will FBOs use this opportunity to proselytise amongst the socially excluded and vulnerable?

It is clearly objectionable when people make the most of someone's social, economic or any other kind of disadvantage to attempt to convert them, just as it's objectionable when people use such disadvantages to make a sale. To defend against such a possibility, should we keep FBOs out of the welfare space, or force them to secularise as the price of entry?

We would suggest not. The FBOs we spoke to – even those with a very explicit faith identity – did not want to 'force' anyone into accepting religious beliefs. The dignity, choice and agency of service-users was respected. They wanted to retain a holistic approach, open to spiritual understandings and responses to the problem – for instance, through

> *In different service contexts, the balance of vulnerability and agency may be very different.*

openly discussing themes like forgiveness in offender rehabilitation or drug treatment programmes.

This is clearly an area in which to avoid abstract or one-size fits all solutions. In different service contexts, the balance of vulnerability and agency may be very different. We have noted above how service users in our experience often find faith-based institutions more supportive and person-focused than some statutory services. FBOs should be encouraged to see that their faith is not only 'not a problem' but an important part of what they can offer service users in the first place. The principle is that the context should be one which accepts vulnerability, but doesn't 'vulnerabilise', making sure that service users have an opportunity to explore their spirituality in the appropriate way.

Again, chaplaincy is one way in which FBOs (including Church of England Schools and Salvation Army hostels) are already doing this, though even their presence is a red flag for hard-line secularists.[10] Ultimately, acknowledging the 'agency' of the service user also means acknowledging the principle of consent. Sports chaplains helpfully describe themselves as 'pastorally pro-active but spiritually re-active', highlighting the need to remain open to the possibility of engagement around spiritual themes, but leaving this open to the instigation of others.

chapter 4 – references

1   George Orwell, *Down and Out in Paris and London* (Penguin, 2013), p. 133.

2   Grace Davie, *Religion in Britain: A Persistent Paradox* (John Wiley and Sons, 2015) p. 208.

3   See http://www.cinnamonnetwork.co.uk/cinnamon-faithaction-audits/ (accessed 19.08.2015).

4   Davie, *Religion in Britain*, p. 206.

5   The British Humanist Association submission to Communities and Local Government Select Committee Localism Inquiry. Available at http://www.publications.parliament.uk/pa/cm201012/cmselect/cmcomloc/547/547cvw11.htm (accessed 19.08.2015).

6   European Court of Human Rights, *Larissis and Others v Greece (140/1996/759/958–960)*, 24 February 1998. Available at http://hudoc.echr.coe.int/eng#{"fulltext":["Larissis"],"documentcollectionid2":["GRANDCHAMBER","CHAMBER"],"itemid":["001-58139"]} (accessed 19.08.2015).

7   A schismatic Christian sect in the fourth and fifth centuries.

8   Kao, *Anti-proselytization*, p. 78.

9   We won't here explore the cases of those in the employ of public bodies (nurses, social workers etc) offering to pray for patients etc, though some of our arguments here would apply.

10 "School chaplains: the Church of England's latest plan to evangelise in schools", National Secular Society, 3 June 2014. Available at http://www.secularism.org.uk/blog/2014/06/school-chaplains--the-church-of-englands-latest-plan-to-evangelise-in-schools (accessed 19.08.2015).

conclusion and recommendations

The issues discussed above reach to the heart of the appropriate scope of religious freedom in a diverse society, and particularly to the terms on which FBOs might engage in offering public services. The term proselytsim, however, is both tendentious and subjectively defined. The chilling effect around the language of proselytism is one of the barriers to the greater participation of FBOs in a diversifying network of providers. We have suggested that the issue is not proselytism itself, but a host of other concerns about what it is for people and organisations of faith to retain that identity in public. Above, we have discussed three – the problems of incivility, diversity, and vulnerability.

This report describes these three key arguments, and suggests that while they deserve attention and reflection, they are not conclusive. First, that civility requires that we work on being able to articulate our beliefs in a moderate way in a plural society; second, that the dignity and integrity of minority groups and cultures requires in fact that we maintain liberty of religious expression, whether against secular or religious orthodoxy and, third, that the argument from vulnerability can result in a situation where we vulnerable-ise service users, and ignore their spiritual needs and spiritual agency.

> *If anything, churches and Christian agencies prefer not to talk about their faith.*

Much of this debate turns, and will continue to turn, on evidential issues. Are FBOs 'forcing' and 'imposing' their beliefs on others? Do they prioritise their own good above the public good? Do they use their position to advocate for controversial social and political views? In the real world, the answer to this question will sometimes be 'yes'. For clarity, however, it's worth saying that a large proportion of FBOs, particularly those in receipt of government funding, had no real agenda to proselytise on any even vaguely non-partisan understanding of the term, not least for their own theological reasons. For many, the concerns are quite the opposite – one interviewee put it to us that, "if anything, churches and Christian agencies prefer not to talk about their faith".

For those that acknowledge that some religious public action is inauthentic or ill-disciplined, then the solution is not to suppress religious identity, but to look to ensure that freedoms are exercised responsibly. We believe that the best practical response to the problem of proselytism is to help agencies be reflective and intentional in their approach.

There is not a one-style-fits-all approach. What we have tended to refer to here as FBOs are heterogeneous in nature: some are worshipping religious communities that additionally have a formal charitable outworking amongst the wider public, while others are charities informed by the religious principles of their founders, and still others are agencies set up to serve a particular need of a particular religious group. They operate at different scales – from the level of community development, through to operating large contracts to deliver public services at scale. They have different relationships with and views of the state and its agencies – some are publicly funded, others are not, and some have formal partnerships, while others are very much 'off the radar'. They are inspired by diverse faith traditions, with different internal structures and 'ecclesiologies'. Even those that come from the same faith tradition think differently about the why, the what and the how of their social action. What we heard again and again in interviews is that the groups should be able to know and articulate what they're about.

> *Even those that come from the same faith tradition think differently about the why, the what, and the how of their social action.*

One charity CEO spoke of their organisation adopting a 'full fat' approach. It's possible to extend the metaphor to offer a category of the different types of approaches.

- Full fat: For these organisations, it's not possible to abstract changes in belief, and membership of a worshipping community, from the 'service' in question, though it is offered to all-comers and seeks to operate within the boundaries of 'informed consent'. They seek to create radical and transformative change, though usually at a small scale because they're unwilling to make the compromises that would come when in receipt of public funding. Success looks like the restoration and transformation of the individual.

- Half fat: These services tend to be embedded or delivered in close partnership with a worshipping community. They aspire to be open to all, and seek to operate with a holistic mission, based on meeting material, social and spiritual needs and their vision of a successful service is rooted in delivering in all three categories. They acknowledge the vulnerability of service users, but will seek to offer and share faith and participation in the life of a worshipping community, with the proviso that the service remains unconditional and non-discriminatory.

- Low fat: The organisation will highly value inclusion, equality and diversity, though usually for theological reasons. It will probably disavow proselytism or evangelism as such, but will see its service users as being on a spiritual journal on which they can and should assist, though sometimes in very passive ways. These groups are more likely to be in receipt of statutory funding, and therefore are subject to and aware of greater regulatory and performance pressures. Success means delivering against targets set within contracts and agreements, albeit in ways informed by their faith-based ethos.

These distinctions are descriptive – we do not recommend one approach against others and, arguably, the most obvious conclusion is that FBOs need to know where they are and where they want to be and how they will manage many of the issues presented in this report. Even though, for instance, vulnerability is an issue, we need to adopt a more individuated approach – not all service-users will be as vulnerable as others, and some indeed may value an opportunity to have a conversation about faith. What is the context? What is the service provided?

> FBOs need to know where they are and where they want to be.

recommendations

Generally speaking, there have been two different responses to these issues amongst FBOs. Those that wish to retain an evangelistic objective tend to operate off the radar – focusing on community-based, privately funded projects which have varying degrees of connection with statutory or third sector partners. Others effectively forswear 'proselytism' through contracting requirements, or by signing statements of intent such as the All Party Parliamentary Group Covenant. These are understandable ways in which trust has to be built, but arguably it's a flawed approach. As we've discussed, it isn't actually clear what this rules out, and seeks to determine in general arrangements which should be made on a case by case basis.

One issue of concern is what about the groups that aren't prepared to sign up to these? It may be right that they should not be in receipt of public funds, but it would be both pointless and wrong to suggest that, though they wish to continue to express their faith, they are necessarily insignificant, harmful, or in other ways illegitimate. It should be remembered that freedom to change one's religion is an Article 9 freedom – without greater freedom when it comes to proselytism and other forms of religious expression, it is at risk of becoming 'a dead letter' in some contexts.

In view of this, we recommend the following:

- Public agencies and FBOs should recognise that there are different approaches – from 'full-' to 'low-fat', which will require different types of relationships. This will move away from a binary approach, which tend to push FBOs 'off the radar', or into a very passive mode where mission becomes merely internal or implicit.

- Covenants, contracts and bidding documents etc., should not adopt a 'thou shalt not' but a 'thou shalt' approach – sometimes, an FBO's aims and ethos will not marry with the objectives of a public body, and sometimes they will. FBOs are not deserving of particular suspicion, and are capable of observing appropriate limits when clear objectives and expectations are set.

> *FBOs are not deserving of particular suspicion, and are capable of observing appropriate limits when clear objectives and expectations are set.*

- Such an approach would highlight values such as transparency, the priority of the public good, attention to spiritual needs and the importance of approaches based on consent. FBOs do need to be honest, explicit and consistent in their approach. Clarity is the basis for relationships of trust between FBOs and funders, commissioners, peer organisations and service users.

- Most of the organisations we spoke to had a clear sense of their own purpose, and how their ethos would be practically expressed, and other FBOs should be supported in explicit conversations around this theme. They need to have reflected on what their objectives are and what approach they will take. As part of this project, we will be providing a resource for FBOs which will support such conversations.

- People are 'spiritual animals', and many services should recognise this to a greater degree. It's right that FBOs acknowledge vulnerability, but they shouldn't vulnerable-ise, talking themselves into a position where it's impossible to recognise the spiritual aspect of people's life and experience. Agencies – faith-based and otherwise – providing services to the public need to incorporate this into the services they hope to offer. There are various non-intrusive ways that this can be done. For example, even secular agencies and projects could make greater use of multi-faith chaplaincy, or work closely with local faith institutions to develop trust-based partnerships.

- More work needs to be done in understanding how FBOs can offer services that bear a rich ethos in ways that reflect the agency and needs of the service user. In the words of another interviewee, "We want people to have the opportunity to ask life questions".

Proselytism has come to be understood and used as a means of restricting religious public action when it should really be used simply as a means of merely disciplining it. As a concept it is useful in alerting us to the possibility of egregious religious public action. But the reality is that there is very little of such activity. If we understand it properly and respond to it maturely the problem of proselytism should be recognised for what it is – no problem at all.